JoJo Loves
BowBow

Cataloging-in-Publication Data has been applied for and may be obtained from the Library of Congress.

ISBN 978-1-4197-3207-2

Jacket illustrations copyright © 2018 Siobhán Gallagher
Book design by Caitlin Keegan

Printed and bound in U.S.A.
10 9 8 7 6 5 4 3 2 1

Amulet Books are available at special discounts when purchased in quantity for premiums and promotions as well as fundraising or educational use. Special editions can also be created to specification. For details, contact specialsales@abramsbooks.com or the address below.

ABRAMS The Art of Books
195 Broadway, New York, NY 10007
abramsbooks.com

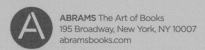

JoJo Loves BowBow

JOJO SIWA

Amulet Books
New York

BOWBOW'S TWO FAVORITE FOODS ARE PIZZA AND CUPCAKES. WE CAN'T FEED HER PIZZA, OF COURSE, BUT WE MAKE DOG-FRIENDLY CUPCAKES AS A SPECIAL TREAT! WHENEVER WE MAKE DOGGIE CUPCAKES, SHE'S RIGHT THERE MAKING THEM WITH US.

xo, JoJo

ONE OF BOWBOW'S FAVORITE THINGS IS GETTING DRESSED
IN THE MORNING. IT'S SO FUNNY—SHE WON'T LET ANYONE
BUT ME PUT CLOTHES ON HER! I DRESS HER ALMOST EVERY SINGLE
DAY. SHE LOVES WEARING HOODIES, JUST LIKE HER MOM—SHE
WANTS TO WEAR HOODIES ALL THE TIME!

xo, JoJo

BOWBOW JUST LOVES TO SIT BY US, SO WE JOKE AROUND AND PUT HER AT THE KITCHEN TABLE IN HER VERY OWN CHAIR. SOMETIMES WE PUT DOG TREATS ON THE TABLE SO SHE CAN REACH UP AND GRAB THEM WITH HER PAWS AND TAKE THEM BACK DOWN TO HER CHAIR.

xo, JoJo

BOWBOW

BOWBOW DOESN'T LIKE HER DOG BED . . . FOR SLEEPING, ANYWAY! SHE IS REALLY GOOD AT HIDING TREATS IN HER DOG BED, THOUGH— THAT IS THE ONLY TIME SHE ENJOYS BEING IN IT. IF SHE'S ON HER BED, WE KNOW SOMETHING'S UP, AND A FEW MINUTES LATER WE'LL FIND FIVE TREATS IN THERE!

xo, JoJo

BOWBOW

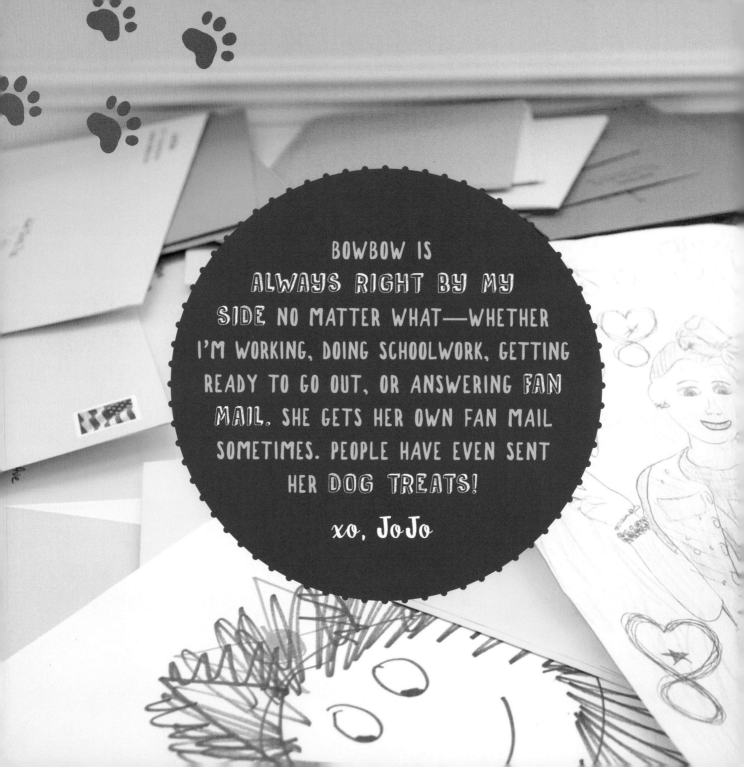

BOWBOW IS ALWAYS RIGHT BY MY SIDE NO MATTER WHAT—WHETHER I'M WORKING, DOING SCHOOLWORK, GETTING READY TO GO OUT, OR ANSWERING FAN MAIL. SHE GETS HER OWN FAN MAIL SOMETIMES. PEOPLE HAVE EVEN SENT HER DOG TREATS!

xo, JoJo

WE USE THE DOG STROLLER IN AIRPORTS AND TO RUN ERRANDS, LIKE WHEN WE GO TO THE STORE. WE TAKE BOWBOW TO THE AIRPORT ALL THE TIME, AND WE TAKE HER ON WALKS IN THE NEIGHBORHOOD—SHE LOVES IT! WHEN SHE'S IN HER STROLLER, SHE LIKES TO HAVE HER LITTLE PAWS ON THE FRONT EDGE OF THE SEAT, LOOKING OUT AT THE WORLD.

xo, JoJo

PEOPLE IN OUR NEIGHBORHOOD LOVE IT WHEN BOWBOW GOES OUT! SHE'S VERY PROTECTIVE OF ME AND ACTS ALL TOUGH, BUT SHE'S REALLY VERY FRIENDLY AND LOVES TO SAY HI TO PEOPLE AND GIVE THEM KISSES!

xo, JoJo

BOWBOW IS IN MOST OF MY VIDEOS. SHE
LOVES BEING ON CAMERA, AS LONG AS I
GIVE HER SOME OF HER FAVORITE TREATS!

xo, JoJo

IF BOWBOW COULD UNDERSTAND HER STAR POWER, SHE'D BE SO EXCITED. SHE LOVES ALL THE ATTENTION. SHE'S A GOOD LITTLE GIRL!

xo, JoJo

BOWBOW DOESN'T RECOGNIZE HERSELF IN MY VIDEOS. ONE TIME, MY BROTHER, JAYDEN, POSTED A VIDEO ON HIS BLOG OF BOWBOW'S BEST DOG FRIEND, MOLLY. MOLLY ALWAYS WEARS BELLS, HER SIGNATURE NOISE—IT'S THE CUTEST THING. BOWBOW HEARD MOLLY'S BELLS ON MY BROTHER'S VIDEO AND GOT REALLY EXCITED, BECAUSE SHE THOUGHT MOLLY WAS RIGHT THERE WITH US!

xo, JoJo

PLAYING OUTSIDE IS ONE OF BOWBOW'S FAVORITE THINGS! SOMETIMES I GET SCARED THAT SHE MIGHT RUN AWAY, OR THAT A BIRD MIGHT COME AFTER HER—SHE'S SO TINY! BUT SHE LOVES BEING OUTSIDE, SO WHENEVER SHE'S OUT THERE, I'M RIGHT BY HER SIDE.

xo, JoJo

BOWBOW IS TWO YEARS OLD!
HER BIRTHDAY IS NOVEMBER 1.

xo, JoJo

IF I GET IN BED AND BOWBOW'S NOT ALREADY RIGHT BY MY SIDE, SHE WILL BARK UNTIL I BRING HER UP ON THE BED. SHE'S LIKE A LITTLE PRINCESS. SHE SLEEPS RIGHT NEXT TO ME WITH HER BODY ALWAYS RESTING ON MY ARM OR MY LEG.

xo, JoJo

BOWBOW CAN DO A LOT OF TRICKS! SHE KNOWS HOW
TO GIVE A HIGH FIVE, SPEAK, AND ROLL OVER. SHE'S EVEN
LEARNING TO "GO NIGHT-NIGHT"—IT'S BASICALLY
PRETENDING TO FALL ASLEEP!

xo, JoJo

BOWBOW'S FAVORITE TOY IS HER BOWBOW STUFFED ANIMAL—SHE LOVES PLAYING WITH HER PLUSH TWIN! WHEN WE WENT TO THE TOY STORE TOGETHER, BOWBOW WAS SO EXCITED TO BE SURROUNDED BY OTHER BOWBOWS. SHE WANTED TO PLAY WITH THEM AND HAVE SO MUCH FUN. IT WAS HARD TO ASK HER TO STAND STILL.

xo, JoJo

BOWBOW LOVES WEARING BOWS! SHE LIKES WEARING TWO BOWS EVEN BETTER THAN ONE, BECAUSE HER NAME IS BOWBOW—THAT'S TWO BOWS!

xo, JoJo

BOWBOW LOVES ALL THE SNUGGLY THINGS IN HER GIANT
WARDROBE, EXCEPT WIGS. SHE PREFERS HER OWN FABULOUS FUR!
WE KEEP HER WARDROBE IN MY BEDROOM. SHE PROBABLY HAS A
HUNDRED DIFFERENT OUTFITS—A LOT OF ONESIES!

xo, JoJo

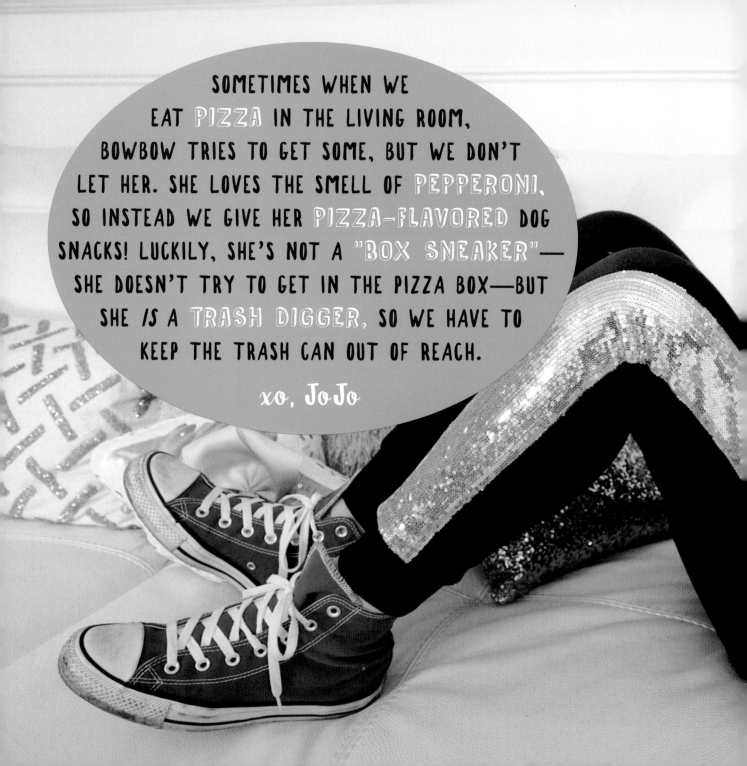

OUR FAMILY LOVES DOING
PUZZLES TOGETHER. OF
COURSE, BOWBOW WANTS TO
HAVE FUN WITH US, SO IT'S
ALWAYS A PARTY. BOWBOW
IS ALWAYS DOING PUZZLES
AND GAMES WITH ME
AND MY MOM—AND MY DAD
AND JAYDEN TOO, IF THEY'RE
IN TOWN VISITING FROM
OMAHA, WHERE JAYDEN IS
FINISHING HIGH SCHOOL.
IT'S ALWAYS FUN
WITH OUR FAMILY!

xo, JoJo

BOWBOW HAS A SPECIAL BOW WITH A TINY BOTTLE OF JUICE IN ITS CENTER FOR JOJO'S JUICE! SHE'S A REGULAR GUEST STAR ON JOJO'S JUICE!

xo, JoJo

SOMETIMES BOWBOW LIKES TO HAVE HER MOM ALL TO HERSELF, BUT SHE LOVES HANGING OUT WITH HER DOG FRIENDS TOO. SHE GOES TO A PLACE IN LOS ANGELES CALLED D.O.G.—IT'S LIKE A DOG PARTY, AND SHE LOVES IT THERE! BOWBOW IS THE WORLD'S BEST DOG!

xo, JoJo